T0131935

SCHOLASTIC CHESS

Made Easy

A SCHOLASTIC GUIDE FOR STUDENTS, COACHES AND PARENTS

MARK M. WOOD, NATIONAL CHESS COACH

Archway Publishing books may be ordered through booksellers or by contacting:

Archway Publishing
1663 Liberty Drive
Bloomington, IN 47403
www.archwaypublishing.com
844-669-3957

ISBN: 978-1-6657-2660-3 (sc)
ISBN: 978-1-6657-2661-0 (e)

Library of Congress Control Number: 2022912500

Print information available on the last page.

Archway Publishing rev. date: 09/06/2023

Contents

The Company Behind the Book:

Mark Wood and his partner Joseph Weber, operated Wood Chess Services as a division of Wood Enrichment Services since 2011. The organization has had twenty-six awards at the state and national level. There have been 102 certified chess players that have learned chess through the organization in the past six years.

These chess activities have been practiced at parties, fairs, carnivals, senior centers and online using state of the art resources, proving that chess can be played anywhere,

This picture has several errors. Can you find them?

Equipment and Set Up

Tournament Legal Sets

There are certain requirements for a set to be legal for a tournament. The king should be between 3 ¾ and 4 ¼ inches tall. The board should have 2 ¼ inch squares. The white and dark pieces and squares should be of sharp contrast. The pieces and the board also must be sized correctly. Four pawns should fit into a square on the board without spaces.

Chess Clocks

Chess clocks are required in most tournaments. The preferred style is a digital with a delay setting. This prevents a losing player from running out the clock and getting an unfair win. They are used for blitz games, quick games and standard tournament games.

The clock should always be pressed with the same hand that moves the piece. Black gets to choose the type and position of the clock.

Setting Up the Board

White pieces are always set up on rows 1 and 2 with a white square on the right corner. White goes first. Each queen is always placed on its own color. If the board is set up incorrectly, within the first ten moves, the game must be redone. If ten or more moves have been made, then the incorrect board must be used throughout the game.

The Pieces

The following six pieces are part of the chess board. When trading pieces, it is important to know their strength to tell if it is a good trade.

Pawn 1 point	Bishop 3 pts.	Queen 9 pts.
Knight 3 pts.	Rook 5 pts.	King 0 pts.

Pawns

There are eight pawns of each color. On the first move, the pawn can only move one or two spaces forward unless capturing. For the rest of the game, the pawn only can move one space forward unless capturing. The pawn cannot move if there is another piece directly in front of it. A pawn can only move diagonally to capture a piece. It can never go backwards or hop over another piece. When it reaches the eighth rank, it can be promoted to a queen, rook, knight or bishop. It is possible to have as many as nine queens on the board on each side by promoting pawns.

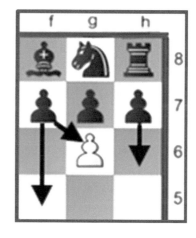

Bishops

There are two bishops of each color. One travels on light squares, one travels on dark squares. Bishops can move diagonally any amount of spaces unless blocked. Bishops cannot jump over other pieces.

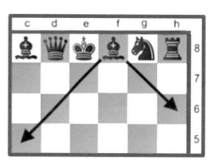

Knights

There are two knights of each color at the start of the game. Knights move in an "L" shape, two spaces one direction and one space another. The knight can hop over pieces but can only take the piece it lands on. In the center of the board, there are eight moves for each knight, only 4 moves if the knight is along the rim.

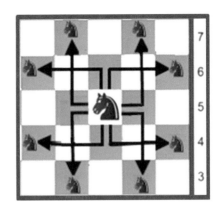

Rooks

There are two rooks of each color at the start of the game. A rook can move sideways, forward, or backwards as many unblocked spaces as possible. The rook my not jump over pieces.

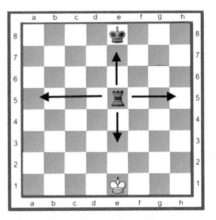

Queen

There is only one queen of each color at the start of the game. A queen can move like the bishop and a rook. It can move diagonally, sideways, forward, or backwards as many unblocked squares as possible. A queen cannot jump over pieces.

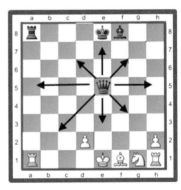

King

There is one king of each color. It can move one square in any direction as long as it is not being threatened. The king cannot jump over pieces. Two kings can never be next to each other. Kings can never be captured in a regular game of chess.

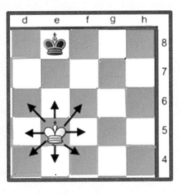

Touch Take Rule- When moving any piece on the board, if a player touches his piece deliberately, it must be moved if legal to do so. If an opponents piece is touched, it needs to be taken, if legal to do so. The rule is ignored if no legal move can be made with the piece. The statement "I adjust" needs to be said when adjusting a piece.

How to Record Moves

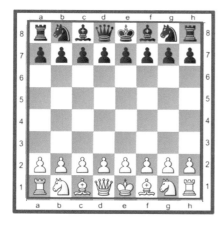

In professional tournaments, recording moves is required unless five minutes or less is shown on either clock in the game.

<u>Capital Letters</u> are used for piece names.

K=King   N=Knight   B=Bishop   Q=Queen
R=Rook   No letter = Pawn

<u>Grid Numbers</u> in small letters are used to designate the destination square. Nc6 means that the knight was moved to square c6. If there is more than one knight that could move to the spot, it could have the designation cNc6. The symbol "e4" shows that the pawn is moved to e4

<u>Miscellaneous Symbols:</u>

A piece taken is shown by an "X" symbol. The symbols "0-0 and "0-0-0" are used for castling. The symbols "+" shows check and "#" designates checkmate. A good move is shown with an exclamation mark, and a question mark indicates a blunder.

1.	e4	e5
2.	Nf3	Nf6
3.	Qe2	Bc5
4.	Nxe5	d6
5.	Nc4	Ng4
6.	f3	Bf2 +
7.	Kd1	Qh4
8.	fxg4	Bxg4
9.	Qxg4	Qxg4+
10.	Be2	Qxg2
11.	d3	Qxh1+
12.	Kd2	Qe1#

Take the sample shown here and play it out on the board. What did the player who played white do wrong in this game?

Openings

Opening Philosophies:

Beginners can get very confused if they are trying to memorize openings. Learning openings is difficult because there are dozens of variations of each one. Instead, follow these basic principles. Never move a piece more than once in the first 6 moves. Control the center of the board. Never charge or "play hero" with your queen. Keep knights toward the center. Avoid tricky moves such as gambits and sacrifices until experienced. Keep pawns staggered on different files. Castle early, preferably king side to access the rook and protect the king. The basic openings and defenses shown are good for beginners.

Spanish Game

The Spanish game is otherwise known as the Ruy-Lopez opening. There are many variations of this opening but they all start up with the same three moves, a most common opening.

1. e4 e5
2. Nf3 Nc6
3. Bb5

The English Opening

White starts out with c4 in this opening. It also has the bishop moving into the corner at g3 so it can cover the whole diagonal (called a fianchetto). It was made famous by Howard Staunton, the player that designed chess pieces.

1. c4 e6
2. Nc3 f5
3. g3 Nf6
4. Bg2

The Italian Game

This is an e4 opening where bishops and knights are developed. The difference is that the bishop only comes out to c4 to provide an attack down the center of the board.

1. e4 e5
2. Nf3 Nc6
3. Bc4

The Vienna Game

The Vienna game is a d4 opening with development of the knight on the Queen side.

1.	d4	nf6
2.	c4	e6
3.	Nf3	d5
4.	Nc3	dXc4

The Center Game

The center game is a favorite of the author. The idea is to control the center of the board with the queen.

e4	e5
d4	eXd4
QXd4	Nc6

Scotch Game

This game is like the center game only the knights are in play sooner. Once again, the Queen controls the center.

1.	e4	e5
2.	Nf3	Nc6
3.	D4	eXd4
4.	nXd4	nXd4
5.	QXd4	----

Queen's Pawn

This is a very simple opening that starts by d4. It controls the center and prevents a Sicilian Defense for Black.

The pawn on d4 controls e5 and the move frees the Bishop on c1 gives the Queen more room to move.

d4 (56%)
or
d4 d5 (28%)

Stonewall Variation

The Stonewall is a variation of the Queen Pawn opening. It involves moving the paws to d4, e3, c3, and f4. It is a closed game that requires patience game. It is a flexible opening that can be done in any order and can develop into other variations.

d4
c3
e3
Bd3
Nd2
Nf3
Nd2
0-0

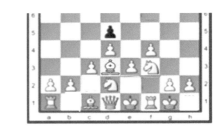

Weber's Backwards Stonewall

The opening is like the Stonewall, but the pawn structure is developed backwards. This opening controls the board center, adds a bishop fiancetto, and makes it easier to develop pieces. Great king protection is shown.

c4
e4
Nc3
g3
bg2
Ne2
0-O

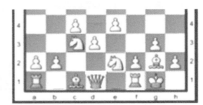

Defenses

French Defense

The strength of this defense is that the pawns are in perfect position for black. There is also good control of the center.

1. e4   e6
2. d4   d5

Fried Liver Attack

The Fried Liver Attack is a variation of the Two Knights Defense. A knight is sacrificed for position. The queen and the bishop push the king out of position for an easy attack.

1. E4   e5
2. Nf3   Nc6
3. Bc4   Nf6
4. Ng5   d5
5. eXd5   NXd5
6. NXf7   KXf7

The Sicilian Defense

This is a common defense used by black when white moves to e4. It helps control the center of the board. After the first few moves, there are many different variations.

1.	e4	c5
2.	Nf3	d6

Caro Kann Defense

This defense is like a Sicilian Defense, but the "c" pawn is only moved out one square.

1.	e4	c6
2.	d4	d5
3.	e5	Bf5

Slav Defense

This defense is used with a d4 opening. This defense helps black defend the d5 pawn and provides good pawn structure.

1.	d4	d5
2.	c4	c6

King's Indian Defense

The King's Indian Defense uses the bishop on a diagonal with the rook at g7 to form a fianchetto. A fianchetto is when a bishop covers a long diagonal. It takes a lot of patience for black and is not good for an aggressive player.

1.	D4	Nf6
2.	c4	d6
3.	Nc3	Bg7
4.	E4	d6

If both bishops are diagonal to the rook, the opening is called a "hippopotamus".

Examining Checks and Checkmates

Check & Checkmate

When the king is put in danger by an opponent, check is called. The king can never remain in check and the <u>king may never be captured</u> in a regular chess game. The opponent must move out of check or the game is over. The object of the game is to get the opponent's king so it cannot legally move while in check. This is called checkmate.

Getting Out of Check

There are three ways to move out of check: Take the threatening piece (1), insert a piece to block the check (2), or move the king into a non-threatening square (3).

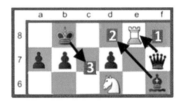

Four Move Checkmate Disasters

The worst type of checkmate to try is the scholar's mate or four move checkmates. Moving the queen out early is a guaranteed loss against a good player. It prevents good opening development. So, unless a player likes having the queen chased all over the board, they could not try it. It is important to know to prevent this mate, because if the center pawn is not guarded, it also can be a quick loss.

Using the Sacrifice as a Checkmate Trick

In this situation, it is black's turn. The white player sacrifices his queen for the checkmate. If black, takes the queen with the rook (RXf5), then the white knight takes the pawn (NXa7#) to form a double check and mate. When taking a valuable piece, always look around and study the situation.

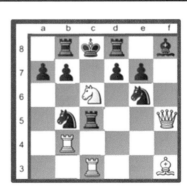

The Tie Game

Stalemate

If no pieces on the board can move legally, but the player is not in check, it is a stalemate.

In the diagram on the right, black is to move. No pieces can move legally. Since there is no check, it is a declared stalemate.

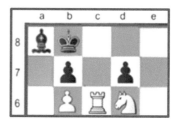

Forced Threefold Repetition

It is a tie if the position on the board is repeated three times. Three repeated moves are forced by the white player who moved first.

23. Rh6+ Kh8 24. Rh7+ Kg8

25. Rh6+ Kh8 26. Rh7+ Kg8

27. Rh6+ Kh8 28. Rh7+ Kg8 (Draw)

Insufficient Material

It is a draw if a player does not have material to checkmate. To checkmate, a player needs at least one of the following five situations:

1. 1 pawn   2. 1 rook   3. 1 queen

4. Two bishops   5. 1 bishop with 1 knight

It is not possible to force a mate with two knights. This position is a tie due to insufficient material.

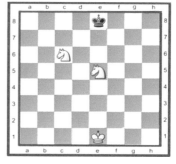

50 move rule

It is a tie if no capture has been made and no pawn has been moved in the last 50 moves. A "move" consists of a player completing their turn followed by the opponent's turn.

Mutual Agreement

Both players can agree to a tie. It is not legal to agree to a draw in the beginning of the game or to prearrange it to secure a championship. (USCF rule 14.b.6)

Forks, Pins, Skewers and Traps

Fork A fork is when a piece is threating two or more pieces at the same time.	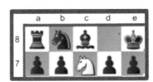
Pin It is a pin when a piece cannot move because a piece behind it is being threatened. In this diagram, the queen cannot move because it is pinned in front of the king.	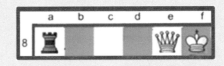
Skewer It is called a skewer when a piece is behind another piece that can be captured if moved.	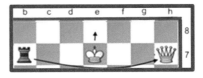
Trap A trap occurs when a piece cannot move without being captured. To prevent traps, try never to put a knight or a bishop on the side of the board. In the picture, the knight is trapped.	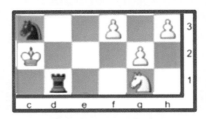

Double Attacks and Double Checks

Double Attack

When one chess piece blocks another, it is possible to move that piece and threaten two pieces at the same time. In this example, the Bishop moves out, takes pawn. Now rook and queen are threatened at the same time

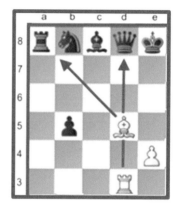

Double Attack with Check

Bishop moves out, takes pawn. Black cannot take the bishop because of the check. White then wins the rook. This can be done using a check with one of the pieces as shown here or with any other two pieces of value.

Double Check

In this example, the rook is moved to check the king. The king is now in check by two pieces. The only way out is to move the king, which is impossible here. It is a checkmate

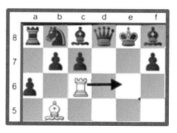

Standard Mating Procedures

A beginner should know how to mate with two rooks, one rook, and one queen. This can be accomplished with practice. Mating with two bishops is somewhat harder, and mating with a knight and a bishop can be accomplished but over 40 moves are needed. For practice in any of these mates, look at the website at https://www.chessvideos.tv/. Specific videos are shown for each mate.

1. **Two Pieces (Rooks and or Queens):** When mating with a combination of two rooks, queens, or both, set the pieces in two columns and push the king to the end of the board. This is called the ladder mate.

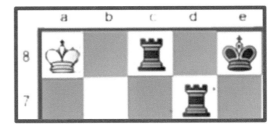

2. **One Rook:** When using one rook, make a box around the king. Make sure the king is always next to the rook. Then force the king into a corner without checking the king at any time. The three pieces make a triangle when checkmated.

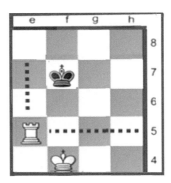 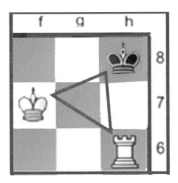

3. **One Queen:** When mating with a queen, push the queen to the rim using the box technique. Once the king is on the rim, move the queen to the row or column in front of the king. Then push the king near the queen and checkmate.

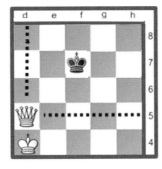 

4. **Two bishops:** When mating with two bishops, start by pushing the king toward the corner using a technique like the ladder mate with two rooks. (1) Then move the king into its proper position which is a knight move away from the corner (2). Get the opponent's king into the corner making sure the king can move. (3)

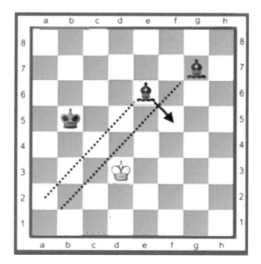

5. **A knight and a bishop:** Mating with a bishop and knight is very hard and takes over 30 moves. The mate must be in the corner that is the same color square as the bishop. Look at the site at https://www.chessvideos.tv for details.

Special Strategies with Pawns

The best way to keep pawns is in a staggered method together. Avoid having pawns stacked in the same column or isolated by themselves.

Good Pawn Structure

Poor Pawn Structure

Mating with Pawns

It is possible to mate with just one pawn using a method called "tempo". The black king must always be in front of the pawn, so it can block. Always move the king and never the pawn unless it is required to prevent capture. The black king's goal is to reach one of two key squares colored in yellow below to promote a pawn to a queen. Here, it is white to move and black can easily promote the pawn.

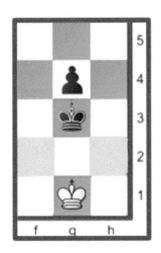

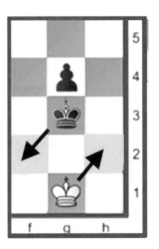

En Passant

On the first move of a pawn, it can move one or two spaces. However, if it moves two spaces to avoid capture with another pawn, that pawn can still be taken, but only on the next opponent's move. The term means "in passing".

Unique Games to Develop

The Pawn Game

This game is set up with all pawns and a king. The object is to learn how to promote pawns efficiently. Two good players should draw this game.

"You Tie, You Lose"

You Tie, You Lose is a game where one side has a king and a rook and the other has a king and a queen. The player with the queen will lose if it is a tie game. The goal of the activity was to learn how to mate with a queen when the opponent has pieces.

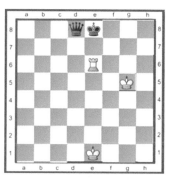

The Zoo

The Zoo is a beginner activity where there are too many pieces on the board, so a player gets confused. It is easy to stalemate without good checkmating skills. The goal is to avoid stalemate by checking continuously.

The Nine Point Game

After a barricade is set up in the center of the board, each player (in secret), puts his king and a combination of pieces that equal exactly nine points anywhere that is legal within the first three rows of his side. The barricade is then removed. White starts first unless black is threatened or in check by the original setup. The goal is to recognize ways to coordinate pieces most effectively.

The Rook Game

The setup on the right is used to develop the Rook's attack. Students learn how to control files with rooks to control the board.

The Knight Game

The goal of the game is to learn how to use knights to back up pawns and effectively lead an attack. Learning basic forking techniques can win a game in any situation.

En Passant or Is It?

The goal is to use an unusual situation on the board where the winning strategy is not obvious. Players finish the game by completing a specific early endgame situation where En Passant situations are present. White moves first in this example.

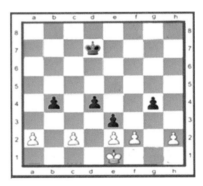

Pawns Vs. Queen

Another unusual situation on the board where the pawns are worth more than a queen. In this example, players finish the game. White also moves first in this example.

Bughouse

This game is played in partners with two speed clocks. One plays with black pieces, and one plays with white pieces on two boards side by side. In each game, when a piece is taken, it is given to the partner. The partner may place the piece anywhere on the board as their move. As soon as one partner wins, both games are over. If a promoted piece is taken, it reverts back to a pawn. A move is not complete until a player's clock is hit.

This game is played in tournaments and has complicated rules. Research would be necessary in order to play correctly.

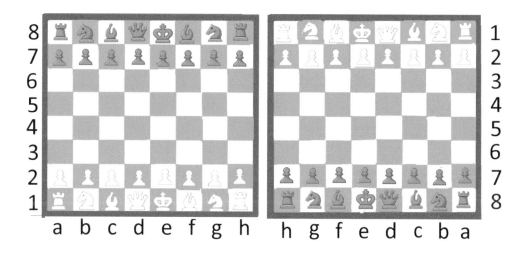

Chess Situation Quiz

Predicting moves by recognizing situations is an important skill in chess. These ten problems require problem-solving skills when applying previous knowledge to new situations. Pick the best most complete answer.

_____ 1. What diagram(s) represents an En Passant situation?

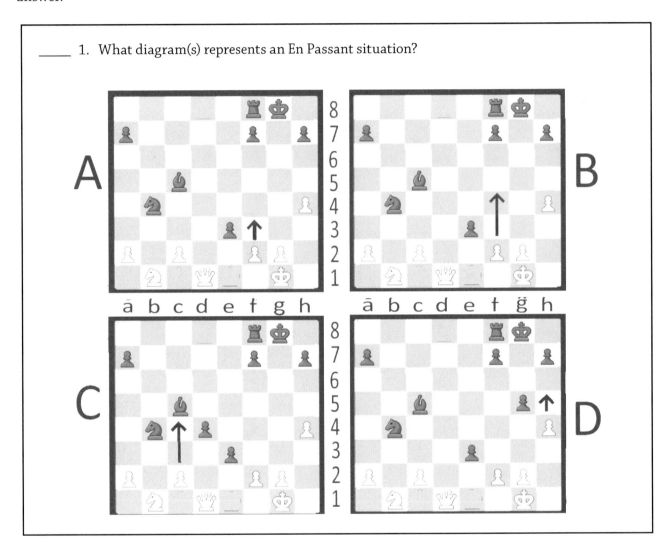

_____ 2. White to move. Which situation(s) will end in a checkmate on the next move?

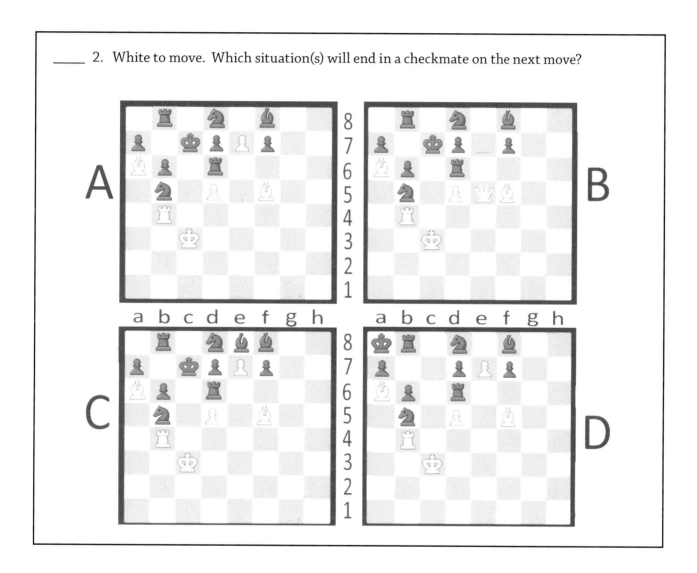

_____ 3. White to move. Which situation(s) will end in a checkmate on the next move.

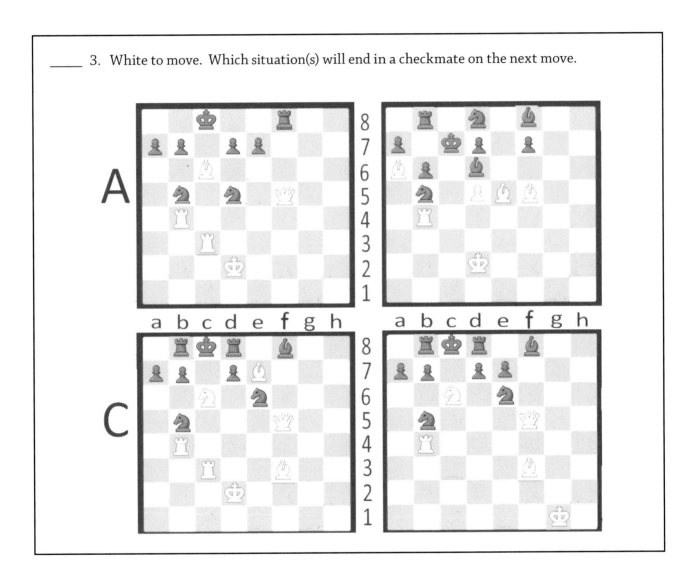

_____ 4. White to move. Which situation(s) will end in a checkmate on the next move.

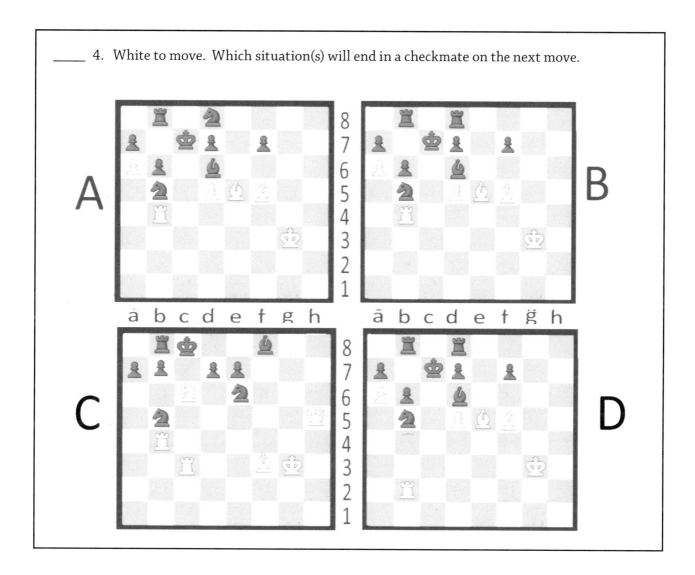

_____ 5. White to move. Which situation(s) will end in a checkmate on the next move.

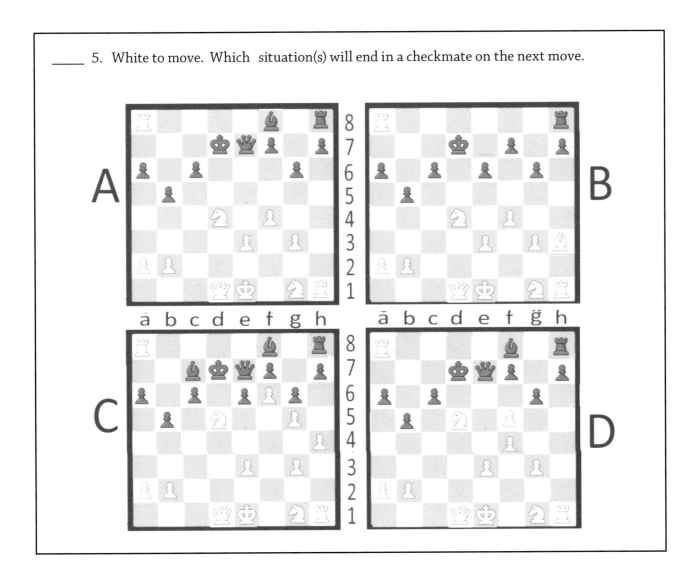

_____ 6. Black to move. Which situation(s) will end in a checkmate on the next move.

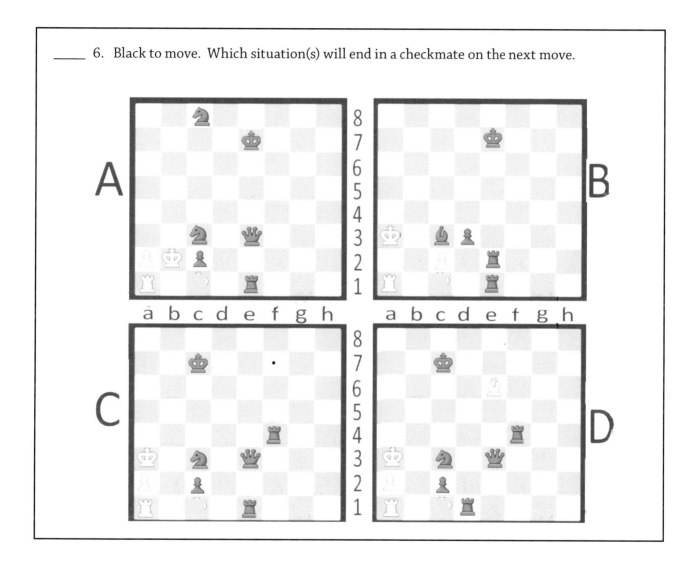

Chess Concept Quiz

_____ 1. Which combination is worth more in points?

    A.   2 Rooks and 3 Pawns   C.   1 Queen and 1 Knight

    B.   2 Bishops and 2 Knights   D.   8 Pawns and 2 Bishops

_____ 2. What can be done to get out of double check?

    A.   Put piece in front of king.   C.   Move King

    B.   Take threating piece   D.   None of the above

_____ 3. What is it called when a piece cannot move without being put in check?

    A.   Skewer.   C.   Pin

    B.   Checkmate.   D.   Double Attacks

_____ 4. When mating with a rook, which of the following is not true?

    A.   Never check the king.   C.   Keep your king near the rook.

    B.   Push the rook on the rim.   D.   Use the box technique to corner the rook.

_____ 5. When using the clock, which of the following is always true?

    A.   Illegal move stops clock.   C.   It has to be digital with delay options.

    B.   White chooses the clock.   D.   It is always hit with the right hand.

_____ 6. Which combination cannot be used to force a checkmate?

    A.   2 bishops   C.   2 knights

    B.   1 pawn   D.   1 knight and one bishop

_____ 7. In which situation can a player still castle?

    A.   The king has moved.   C.   The castling rook is being threatened

    B.   The player is in check.   D.   The castling rook has been moved

_____ 8. When recording, what does the symbol "0-0 mean?

    A.   En Passant   C.   Long Side Castling

    B.   Fianchetto   D.   King Side Castling

_____ 9. Which can cause an instant loss because of poor sportsmanship?

    A.   Not shaking hands.   C.   Opponent offers draw before game.

    B.   Not saying check.   D.   Letting player's clock run down.

___ 10. What is another name for the Spanish game?

    A.   Fried Liver Attack.   C.   Caro Kann Defense.

    B.   The Center Game   D.   Ruy Lopez Opening.

___ 11. Which is not a type of opening?

    A.   Hippopotamus   C.   Dragon

    B.   Fried Liver   D.   Rattlesnake

___ 12. How many total queens are possible in a chess game?

    A.   2   C.   9.

    B.   4   D.   18.

___ 13. What does the French statement "En Passant" really mean?

    A.   Hidden Capture   C.   In Passing

    B.   Pawn Promotion   D.   None of the Above.

___ 14. Which of the following is considered legal equipment in a tournament?

    A.   Analog Clock   C.   2-inch diameter pawn on a 2-inch square.

    B.   Pieces of all similar colors   D.   Travel Chess Set with Roman Pieces

___ 15. In what situation are you required to record in a major tournament? game?

    A.   Game has 4:53 left by opponent, player has 6:02   C.   In a Blitz game.

    B.   Both players have 4:00 left on the clock.   D.   None of the Above

16 - 20   Name five different ways to draw a game:

    16. _____ 17. _____,

    18._____ 19. _____.

    20. _____.

21- 23   Name three different ways to get out of a check:

    21. _____ 22 _____ 23. _____

24-25 Give two examples of good sportsmanship during a chess game.

    24. _____.

    25. _____.

Chess Crossword Challenge

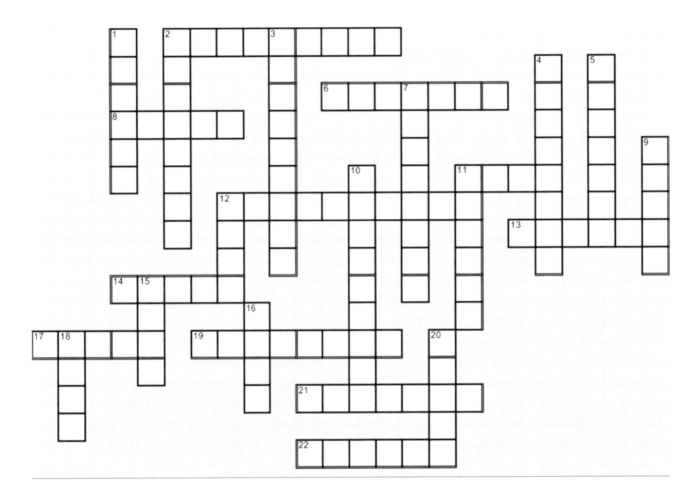

Across

2 Type of draw.

6 The _____ opening is another name for the Ruy Lopez .

8 Fast game done in 10 minute.

11 Insufficient Material

12 Move with Bishop to control diagonal.

13 Two of these cannot force a mate.

14 Digital or Analog

17 Piece that is worth 9 points.

19 Style of piece used in tournaments

21 Last 10 moves of the game

22 Reverse of a pin

Down

1 An opening where a player makes a sacrifice.

2 Defense where first move is c5 when playing black.

3 Two words meaning "In Passing".

4 Forced to make a bad move.

5 First moves of a game.

7 Algebraic

9 How many moves is required for a draw if no capture has been made and no pawn has been moved?

10 In _____ repetition, a player claims a draw because of repeated moves.

11 The only way out of _____ check is to move the king.

12 Threatening two pieces at the same time.

15 Another name for queen side castling is _____ side castling

16 Piece is worth 1 point.

18 United States Chess Federation

20 First name of grandmaster who broke records blindfolded.

Answer Key

Chess Situation Quiz

1	C	Pawn moves 2 spaces to avoid capture.	4.	B	Rc4# because the bishop is pinned.
2.	A	Pawn on e7 is promoted to a knight!	5.	C	Nb6# It is a double check.
3.	C	NXa7# or NXc7# Double Check	6.	C	Nd1# - Discovered check and mate

Chess Concept Quiz

1-15   1) D 2) C 3) C 4) B 5) A 6) C 7) C 8) D 9) C 10) D 11) D 12) D 13) C 14) A 15) D

16 – 20 1. Stalemate, 2. Insufficient Material, 3. Threefold Repetition, 4. 50 Move Rule, 5. Agreement

21-23   Move King, Place piece in the way, Take piece.

24 – 25 Any reasonable answer such as shaking hands before and after game, congratulating player, telling player clock is running, making no annoying sounds, reviewing game after match is over, helping player record win, letting player look at scoresheet in order to correct mistakes, helping with setting the clock, not making excessive draw offers, etc.

Crossword Puzzle

ACROSS: (2) Stalemate (6) Spanish (8) Blitz (11) Draw (12) Fianchetto (13) Knight (14) Clock (17) Queen (19) Staunton (21) Endgame (22) Fork

DOWN: (1) Gambit (2) Sicilian (3) en passant (4) Zugwang (5) Opening (7) Notation (9) Fifty (10) Threefold (11) Double (12) Fork (15) Long (16) Pawn (18) USCF (20) Timur

56 Question Assessment, Advanced 56 -51 Proficient 50 - 45 Basic 44-39 Below Basic Under 39

Resources

Openings. (2018). Retrieved from https://www.chess.com/openings

Chess Videos TV - The Largest Chess Video Site on the Web! (2018) Retrieved from https://www.chessvideos.tv/

Crossword Puzzle Maker: (2018). Retrieved from https://crosswordhobbyist.com/

Just, T. (2014). *U.S. Chess Federation's Official Rules of Chess, 6th Edition.* New York: Random House.

Wood Chess of Central Pennsylvania. (2018). Retrieved from https://woodchess.org/

Wood, M. M. (2004). *Beyond Classroom Enrichment: Creative units for Gifted Students. Virginia: Gifted Press*

Printed in the United States
by Baker & Taylor Publisher Services